BEAUTIFUL CATS

PORTRAITS

of

CHAMPION BREEDS

BEAUTIFUL CATS

PORTRAITS

of

CHAMPION BREEDS

by DARLENE ARDEN & NICK MAYS
photographed by ANDREW PERRIS

Ivy Press

First published in the UK in 2014 by

Ivy Press
210 High Street
Lewes
East Sussex BN7 2NS
United Kingdom
www.ivypress.co.uk

British Library Cataloguing-in-Publication Data
A catalogue record for this book is available from the British Library

ISBN: 978-1-78240-106-3

This book was conceived, designed and produced by

Ivy Press
Creative Director **Peter Bridgewater**
Publisher **Susan Kelly**
Editorial Director **Tom Kitch**
Art Director **James Lawrence**
Designer **Ginny Zeal**
Photographer **Andrew Perris**
Illustrator **David Anstey**

Printed in China
Colour origination by Ivy Press Reprographics
10 9 8 7 6 5 4 3 2 1

Distributed worldwide (except North America) by Thames & Hudson Ltd,
181A High Holborn, London WC1V 7QX, United Kingdom

C O N T E N T S

INTRODUCTION

IS THERE ANYTHING IN THE WORLD MORE BEAUTIFUL than a cat? Whether on the move, sleeping or sitting perfectly still, a cat is incredibly lovely to look at. Even the most awkward cat still manages to look graceful. No matter what body or coat type it has, it manages to look like living art.

Beyond its looks, there is a sweetness that nearly defies description. These are the companions that sit quietly beside you, curl up on your lap or make you laugh with their antics, whether engaging in play by themselves or with their human companion.

A cat's purr has healing properties for itself as well as its owners. Its delightfully soft fur is just right for cuddling and petting and its sandpaper kisses are never to be forgotten.

Cats come in a variety of different sizes, shapes and colours as well as coat lengths. Their personalities vary, as do their voices. Some cats are highly vocal and like nothing more than to tell you all about their day, while others have a silent meow – the mouth opens but the pitch is so high that the human ear cannot hear it.

Cats will knead their paws on their owner's lap. Some people call it 'making biscuits', and wonder why they do it. It goes back to when they were very young kittens, when they would use this movement in order to get their mother's milk to flow. It's a high compliment when a cat feels comfortable enough to treat their person the way they treated their mother. It's a form of bonding and love and demonstrates complete confidence in the shared relationship. Is it any wonder that these companions have been loved for centuries?

Whether they are anxiously awaiting their person's arrival home from work at the end of the day, following their person from room to room or 'helping' with the

Above: The sight of a contented cat can be very calming in itself; it is hard to be anxious while watching a cat sleep.

laundry, cats are not the aloof creatures they are often purported to be by observers who don't understand them. On the contrary, they love to be with their family members and, when they're not napping – which adult cats do most of the day – they want to be where the action is, even if this only involves their person reading a book or watching television. A cat is a companion for all seasons and all reasons.

THE EVOLUTION OF THE CAT

THE BIOLOGICAL FAMILY OF CATS IS KNOWN AS felidae. This is divided into two parts: the pantherinae, which includes lions, tigers, jaguars and leopards and snow leopards; and felinae, which includes ocelots, cougars, cheetahs, lynxes, wildcats and the domestic cat. In prehistoric times, there were sabre-toothed cats from a now-extinct third part of the felidae family, machairodontinae. These early cats were obligate carnivores – meaning they survived on a diet mainly of meat – as are today's domestic cats.

Our understanding of the evolution of cats has greatly increased in recent years through the work of geneticists. An article published in 2006 in the journal *Science* examined the results of a study of the DNA of 37 living species of felidae, which confirmed that the subfamilies pantherinae and felinae can be divided into eight distinct lineages. The researchers, led by Warren E. Johnson and Stephen J. O'Brien, drew a family tree and assigned the various cats to these lineages.

The first extant lineage to split from the prehistoric *Pseudaelurus* cats was pantherinae; this occured around 10.8 million years ago. The pantherinae lineage is made up of the genera *Panthera*, *Neofelis* and *Uncia*. Due to the unique structure of their larynx and their flexible hyoid bone, lions, tigers, jaguars and leopards are the only cats that can roar.

The researchers also proposed that there were at least ten intercontinental migrations of these various cat lineages. Being excellent predators, they survived quite well wherever they went. One of the earliest migrations occurred between 8 and 8.5 million years ago, when cats migrated from Asia to North America by crossing the Bering land bridge. In turn, direct ancestors of later lineages crossed from North America back into Eurasia.

The most recent lineage to develop was *Felis*, which includes the wildcat (*Felis silvestris*) and the modern domestic cat (*Felis catus* or *Felis silvestris catus*). Domestic cats have much in common with their wild ancestors. Our housecats still have flexible bodies, move quickly and are great hunters. But thousands of years of living near and among humans has also turned them into wonderful companions for people.

Above: Like its wild ancestor, today's *Felis catus*, or domestic cat, is often an agile and successful hunter.

A HISTORY OF CATS & HUMANS

IT IS THOUGHT THAT CATS FIRST STARTED TO LIVE alongside humans around 10,000 years ago in Southwest Asia, when agriculture was in its early days, or established enough to be attractive to cats. Always intelligent, cats began to make their homes near people to be near the food supply as well as mice and scraps of food. Their prowess in keeping down the rodent population would certainly have been attractive to the people the cats placed themselves near.

The earliest archaelogical evidence of cats living with humans is a gravesite from around 7,500 BCE (the Neolithic Period). The gravesite was discovered in Cyprus. It contained the skeleton of a human and that of a young cat, buried at the same time, and a number of other offerings.

It is well known that cats were worshipped as gods in Egypt. The ancient Egyptians thought that the rays of the sun were kept in cats' eyes at night for safekeeping.

Similarly, though not to quite the same extent as in Egypt, cats were held in high regard in Ancient Rome, and were the only animals allowed to walk freely around temples.

Above: Cats have been more than companions to some; in Ancient Egypt they were worshipped as gods.

However, in some later periods of European history, cats have suffered greatly at the hands of humans. In the Middle Ages cats were considered to be in cahoots with the devil and were killed in great numbers. Sadly this had grave consequences during the Black Death, when a thriving cat population could have killed he rats that were carrying the infected fleas – if only anyone had realized it. Later, during the Renaissance, many thought that cats were witches' familiars, leading to cats being killed in large numbers.

Although it is not known exactly when domestic cats first arrived in the Far East, some estimate it was around 2,000 years ago, and the cats were soon appreciated for both their mousing prowess and their companionship.

Several distinct Oriental breeds developed, including what we now call the KHAO MANEE, BURMESE, SIAMESE and KORAT. They were all described in the *Tamra Maew*, a collection of cat poems written by Buddhist monks during the Ayudhya period. In time, these breeds were to become equally admired in the West with the rise in popularity of the Cat Fancy.

A HISTORY OF THE CAT FANCY

FROM THE LATE SEVENTEENTH CENTURY ONWARDS, cats were back in favour in the West. Their value as vermin killers was appreciated and notions of them as witches' familiars began to fade into the stuff of folklore and fairytales. Crucially, cats began to take on another role as well as their practical one – people began to admire them as companion animals – and thus cats became pets.

In the UK, during the latter half of the nineteenth century, cats soon joined the ranks of domesticated dogs, rabbits, cavies, mice and rats that were being perceived as desirable exhibition animals – and thus the Cat Fancy came into being.

The earliest 'fancy' breeds included the RUSSIAN BLUE, SIAMESE and, of course, the PERSIAN. Certainly there was enough interest in exhibiting cats for the first cat show to be staged in 1868, at London's Crystal Palace. Organized by naturalist and cat lover Fred Wilson, that first show attracted sixty-five exhibits and was deemed to be highly successful.

Thereafter, other shows followed, with the first 'offi-cial' cat show taking place on 13 July, 1871. This show was organized by the famous artist Harrison Weir, assisted by Fred Wilson. In 1887, the National Cat Club was founded by Weir, who became Club President. Another famous founder member was the celebrated artist Louis Wain, whose paintings of anthromorphic cats are still widely known and loved today. The National Cat Club's annual show is held to this day.

It has to be said that the breeding and showing of cats was very much the preserve of the more well-to-do tiers of Victorian society in the UK. Amongst the prime movers of the fledgling Cat Fancy were the Baroness Burdett Coutts and the Duchess of Sutherland. Photographs from early cat shows show the pampered felines sitting on velvet cushions or being led around a ring on leads by well-heeled ladies in expensive dresses and big hats.

The great Charles Cruft of Crufts Dog Show fame even flirted briefly with staging cat shows. Two Crufts for Cats were staged in 1894 and 1895, but failed to generate a profit for Mr Cruft, so he withdrew his patronage.

Above: The origins of cat shows date back to the late nineteenth century; this 1872 print is of London's Crystal Palace exhibition.

Other cat clubs were formed, including many of the first specialist breed clubs. The National Cat Club acted as the main registering body for all pedigree cats. However, disagreements led to several rival registries being founded. The matter was resolved in 1910 when all the registries combined to form the Governing Council of the Cat Fancy (GCCF).

The GCCF remains the majority cat registry in the UK to this day, with over fifteen cat clubs affiliated to it. The GCCF stages its own annual show, the Supreme Cat Show.

The Cat Fancy soon crossed the Atlantic. The Chicago Cat Show staged in 1899 resulted in the formation of the Chicago Cat Club and soon afterwards the powerful Beresford Cat Club, named after British cat fancier Lady Marcus Beresford, proving that an Old World hereditary title still had a certain cachet in the Land of the Free.

A registering body was founded in 1906 as the American Cat Association, which, two years later, changed its name to the Cat Fanciers' Association, Inc, or CFA, and this remains the leading cat registry in the USA today.

Above: Four Persian Blues being groomed by their owners for a championship show at Holy Trinity Hall, London, in 1937.

In 1949, a group of European cat registries formed the Fédération Internationale Féline (FIFe), which swiftly became a worldwide federation of member cat registries and is today the largest in the world.

In 1979, a new, international registry based in the USA was founded, namely The International Cat Association (TICA), which has grown massively in influence and has many member clubs worldwide.

In the twenty-first century, there are cat clubs and registries the world over. In fact, on any weekend of the year, there will be several cat shows taking place somewhere in the world and many in the same country.

In 1994, the World Cat Congress (WCC) was established as an international coordinating organization for the largest worldwide cat registries. The WCC operates an 'open door' policy whereby cats registered with one registry may be shown under the rules of another registry. Needless to say, this egalitarian approach isn't universally subscribed to and some registries refuse to recognize others. The cats, however, couldn't care less one way or the other.

CAT SHOWS IN THE TWENTY-FIRST CENTURY

THERE MAY COME A POINT IN YOUR LIFE AS A CAT owner when you think it would be a marvellous idea to enter your cat in a cat show, whether you own a pedigree or a crossbreed or even 'just' a moggy. Oh yes – ordinary pet cats can rub shoulders (metaphorically speaking) with the upper echelons of the pedigree feline fraternity. In fact, nearly every cat show has a class for 'Household Pets or 'Non Pedigrees'.

Going to a cat show for the first time may seem a daunting prospect, but like any new endeavour, you just need to do a little research beforehand, and then jump in. Once you've worked out the key factors about the show – where, when, which cat to enter and how much it will cost – you are sure to find it to be a fascinating and fun experience.

So, the first things you need to check when entering your cat in a show are the show's location, which club is running it and, crucially, under which registry's rules the show is being held. Nowadays, show information almost always appears on the Internet, with contact details for the show manager or secretary, the show's location

Above: Shows are fun, fascinating and open to all, including pedigrees or your own run-of-the-household cat.

and, importantly, when entries have to be received by, so we won't go into the finer detail here – each club and registry will have its own rules. Usually, the main cat registries and clubs provide helpful 'how to show' guides online for new exhibitors.

As to the way shows are actually judged, this is down to the rules of each registry. For example, some registries such as the CFA and TICA shows use the 'judging ring' system, where the judging takes place in designated areas – the 'rings'. The cats are called in pen number order to be judged and are brought from their show pens to the judging ring pens by either the exhibitor or a steward.

At GCCF shows, the judges walk to each pen and judge the cats on a portable judging table trolley. Each judge is assisted by a steward. Later in the day, prizes are allocated – usually prize cards, rosettes or ribbons and sometimes even prize money.

So go to the show and see how your cat fares but remember – at the end of the day, whatever placings the judge gives out, the best cat – yours – goes home with you.

WHAT IS THE JUDGE LOOKING FOR?

IT ALL LOOKS SO COMPLICATED, DOESN'T IT? YOU'RE at a cat show, watching those judges, resplendent in their white coats or tabards, picking the cats up, running their hands over them, and talking gravely to their steward or assistant, with copious notes being written on the paperwork relating to that cat. What are they looking for? How are the cats actually being judged?

Each cat breed has its own 'standard'. This is a description of observable characteristics and physical attributes such as body shape (known as 'type') and markings. A scale of points based on the ideal cat for that breed is allocated to each of these characteristics and attributes. The breed standards are laid down by the individual cat registries, agreed by the breeders and breed councils and amended and developed over time.

So the judges will be working their way through all the cats entered in a given breed class at a show to see which of the cats entered in that class best conforms to the breed standard. In this way, you will see judges picking the cats up, carefully gauging the cat's physique, checking its coat and conformation to

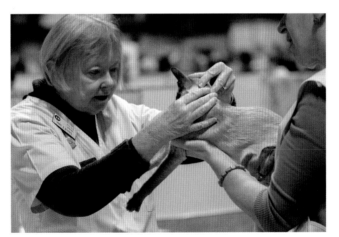

Above: A judge examines a cat with care, checking for markings and good health and comparing it to the breed standard.

colour or markings. They will also do a general 'once over' inspection of the cat's general bodily health – eyes, ears, teeth, paws and claws, legs, tail and so on.

Of course, all cats are checked by a vet before even getting into the show, but sometimes things can be missed, or the cat might start to feel ill during the course of the show, in which case the duty vet is called to assess whether the cat is fit to carry on.

Each cat is then awarded a place corresponding to how well they fit the breed standard.

At larger shows, the winning cats from each breed (Best of Breed) or overall category (Longhairs, Orientals and so on) will compete against each other, with the winner taking the coveted Best In Show title.

In the case of non-pedigree 'Household Pet' cats, the judge will not be referring to a written breed standard, but instead will be looking for a cat with good 'pet characteristics' – a friendly, happy cat that enjoys being handled, is handsome or pretty, in good health and is nicely presented – whether it's a tabby, a black-and-white long-hair or a tortoiseshell.

THE CATS

Striped, spotted, with coats of many colours, SHORTHAIRS AND LONGHAIRS, toms and queens, *calm and coquettish,* docile and vocal, lively and laid-back, MISCHIEVOUS MOUSERS and *loving lap-cats:* it's time to meet and greet our stunning catalogue of 40 of the FINEST FELINE MODELS – all at one stroke! These are definitely the CAT'S WHISKERS.

MAINE COON

TOM

The MAINE COON, one of North America's oldest natural breeds, was first recorded in cat literature in 1861 and was established as a breed over a hundred years ago. Assorted legends surround this cat's ancestors: one is that because its most common colour is the brown tabby, the breed began when a cat mated with a raccoon – an impossible but funny idea. It is Maine's official state cat.

Features

This 'gentle giant' of cats is distinguished by its large size, tufted ears and snowshoe-like feet. All of this extra fur, including a famously long, bushy tail in which it can wrap itself, keeps the cat warm and allows it to walk lightly in the New England snow. Maine Coons come in about 75 different colour combinations and can have brown or blue eyes, or one of each.

Temperament

This breed likes children, other pets and is famed for its sweet disposition. It remains kittenish and enjoys playing fetch. An intelligent cat, it loves following its owners around and will not only play in water, but sometimes wash its food in it.

Similar breeds

Norwegian Forest Cat, Siberian, Turkish Van

Size

Tom .... 6–8 kg/13–18 lb

Queen ... 4–6 kg/9–13 lb

Origin

The Maine Coon was a wild cat found in Maine. The breed almost died out in the mid-twentieth century, but since then it has seen such a revival in interest that it is now the third most popular cat in the USA. It was first imported into the UK in 1984.

USA

RAGDOLL

T O M

The RAGDOLL is something of an enigma. This beautiful, large, longhaired cat seems to have a special gene that makes it laidback and relaxed in nature. Pick up a Ragdoll and it will usually go limp and floppy, just like a rag doll.

Features

This cat has a large, muscular body and striking, bright-blue eyes. Its plush, medium-length coat has coloured points, including seal, chocolate, cream and tortie, to the face, ears, legs and tail. The Mitted Ragdoll has white front feet, white back hocks and a natty white chin. The Bi-Colour Ragdoll has more white on its legs and body and a white 'V' marking on its face.

Temperament

Very docile, affectionate and laidback, the Ragdoll is not a very vocal cat and positively enjoys being carried around, flopping contentedly in its owner's arms. It will play happily and even learn to fetch in a dog-like way, and it mixes well with dogs and children.

Similar breeds

Birman, Snowshoe

Size

Tom .... 7–9 kg/15–20 lb

Queen ... 5–7 kg/11–15 lb

Origin

The Ragdoll originated in California, USA, in the early 1960s with a white longhaired female named Josephine. The story goes that Josephine was hit by a car, and after her recovery all litters born to her had limp, docile personalities – though this is genetically impossible.

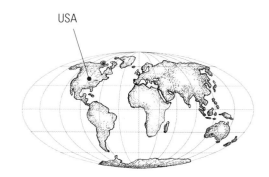

USA

KURILIAN BOBTAIL
QUEEN

Not surprisingly, the KURILIAN BOBTAIL derives its name from its bobbed tail, the fluffy, pom-pom shape which is caused by the reduced number of vertebrae. Despite its 'wild' appearance, it is a gentle, sweet-natured and playful cat that is highly valued in Russia as a good mouser. Although it is a naturally occurring breed, the Kurilian is not recognized by all cat registries.

Features

This is a well-muscled, medium- to large-sized cat, semi-cobby and broadchested. It has a large, slightly wedge-shaped head and 'walnut-shaped' eyes (oval at the top, rounded at the bottom), with ears that slope slightly forwards. Its defining feature is, of course, its rounded bobtail. The breed can be short or semi-longhaired and is bred in a diverse range of colours and markings.

Temperament

The Kurilian Bobtail is very person orientated and will give and seek affection in equal measure. It is highly intelligent, inquisitive and playful, and enjoys playing in water. It mixes well with other animals and makes a perfect family pet.

Similar breeds

Cymric, Japanese Bobtail, Karelian Bobtail, Manx

Size

Tom .... 5–7 kg/11–15 lb

Queen ... 3–5 kg/7–11 lb

Origin

The Kurilian originated on Eastern Russia, the island of Sakhalin and the adjacent Kuril Islands. The breed has slowly gained popularity in Europe but it is only within the late-twentieth century that it made an appearance in North America, where its numbers are still very limited.

Kuril Islands, Sakhalin
& Eastern Russia

SELKIRK REX
QUEEN

Did you ever see a stuffed animal walking? You'll think so when you first see a SELKIRK REX. The curly coat, which can be shorthaired and longhaired, is as snuggly as it looks. Unlike the Cornish or Devon Rex, the rex gene (which causes the coat's curliness) in this breed is dominant. It was first seen in a kitten from a cat adopted from an animal shelter in the USA.

Features

The Selkirk Rex is a heavy boned, medium- to large-sized cat. It comes in an array of colours, with round eyes and a sweet expression that equates with its personality. But its star features are its tousled hair, curly whiskers and plush coat – the shorthaired variety's is more like a teddy bear while that of the longhaired variety more closely resembles a sheep's coat. In the show ring there are two divisions for the Selkirk Rex based upon the coat length.

Temperament

With its sweet, patient and laid-back personality, the Selkirk Rex makes a lovely and surprisingly playful companion.

Similar breeds

Cornish Rex, Devon Rex, LaPerm, Persian, Sphynx

Size

Tom.......5–7 kg/11–15 lb

Queen...2.5–5.5 kg/6–12 lb

Origin

This breed originated in Montana, USA in the 1980s, when one of the five offspring of a blue tortie and white feral mother sprouted curly hair and whiskers. When fourteen months old, this kitten was bred to a black male Persian – half of the litter produced curly haired kittens.

USA

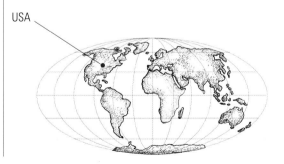

BENGAL
QUEEN

The strikingly beautiful and clever BENGAL is the result of the first deliberate effort to create a domestic cat using a wild cat. With its sleek elegance, lithe body and exquisite 'wild cat' markings, this cat – which has a flight/flight reaction rather than fight or flight – has many admirers.

Features

The Bengal's short, soft coat is its crowning glory. The markings are usually very vivid spots or marbelling, or it could have rosettes much like jaguars, leopards and ocelots. Some even have 'glitter', which gives each hair an iridescent sheen. The popular black/brown tabby's coat can be anything from gold and bronze to grey, while a form of albinism results in blue or aqua eyes and a cream or ivory coat with spots of varying shades.

Temperament

Loving, curious, and with almost frightening intelligence and energy, the Bengal wants to be where you are. This cat loves playing games and, when tired enough, enjoys sitting on its owner's lap. Many Bengals prefer to drink running water and some will even 'talk'.

Similar breeds

Burmese, Korat, Khao Manee, Siamese, Tonkinese

Size

Tom .... 4–7 kg/9–15 lb

Queen ... 2.5–5.5 kg/6–12 lb

Origin

The Bengal's wild origins go back to the Asian Leopard Cat, which was crossed with a domestic cat in the 1960s by American breeder Jean S. Mill. Today's Bengals trace to the ones Mrs Mill began breeding in the early 1980s. The breed has since been developed by dedicated Bengal breeders around the world.

USA

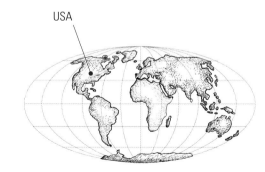

TURKISH VAN

TOM

The Turkish Van is a striking, semi-longhaired breed that originated, as its name suggests, in Turkey. The breed is certainly ancient, as carvings, jewellery and ornaments dating back to the Hittites circa 1600 BCE have been uncovered, depicting cats with distinctive ringed tails and colour on their heads. This breed is also known as the 'swimming cat' because of its notable swimming prowess.

Features

A solid, muscular cat with long, silky soft fur and a thick brush of a tail, a Turkish Van's most distinctive features are its white body and 'van' patterning on its head and tail. The most common marking colour is auburn, although it can be bred in a range of other colours.

Temperament

The Turkish Van is loving, intelligent, very active and dog-like. It will follow its owner devotedly and will enjoy games of fetch with balls, toys or rolled up scraps of paper. With its waterproof coat, this breed will also happily swim in ponds or swimming pools, even joining owners in the bath or shower!

Similar breeds

Maine Coon, Norwegian Forest Cat, Siberian

Size

Tom.......5.5–7.5 kg/12–16 lb

Queen...5.5–6.5 kg/12–14 lb

Origin

The Turkish Van originated around Lake Van, the largest lake in Turkey, where it lived in isolation for centuries until discovered by two British photographers, Laura Lushington and Sonia Halliday, in the mid-1950s. The two women took two kittens back with them to the UK, and the breed was imported to the USA soon thereafter.

Turkey

EGYPTIAN MAU
QUEEN

Whilst fans of many of the older cat breeds are fond of saying that their breed dates back to ancient Egypt, the EGYPTIAN MAU is the one breed that can justifiably claim this honour. It is a naturally occurring breed in the region and its ancestors are depicted in artwork dating back 3,000 years. In fact, these highly intelligent cats were used as hunting animals long before they were revered as gods.

Features

This breed has a striking, spotted shorthaired coat. It has a small- to medium-sized body, slender yet muscular. The head is a slightly rounded wedge shape, with medium to large ears and large, expressive green eyes. The coat is spotted and barred, and bred in three colours: silver, bronze and smoke. It has a distinctive dark dorsal stripe.

Temperament

This intelligent yet sensitive cat develops a close bond with its owner, seeking attention and reassurance and displaying great loyalty. The Mau is known for its distinctive vocalization – it 'chirrups', the pitch conveying its feelings.

Similar breeds

Abyssinian, American Shorthair, Ocicat, Siamese

Size

Tom .... 3.5–5 kg/8–11 lb

Queen ... 2.5–3.5 kg/5–8 lb

Origin

This ancient breed from Egypt was first exported in 1952 when a kitten was given to an exiled Russian princess by the Egyptian ambassador to Italy. The cat was imported into the USA in 1956 and subsequently outcrossed to similar breeds to produce the basis of the modern Mau. The first Maus were imported to the UK in the 1970s.

Egypt

ABYSSINIAN
TOM

The Abyssinian is a cat of exceptional grace and beauty; this is summed up delightfully in TICA's breed description as a cat resembling 'a small mountain lion or cougar'. Certainly it is a very ancient breed, originaly believed to come from Abyssinia (now Ethiopia), although genetic studies have now placed the cat's origin as being in the region of the Bay of Bengal, India.

Features

A medium-sized cat with a long, lithe body and subtle musculature, this breed has a 'modified' wedge-shaped head, with large, erect ears that tilt forward slightly. Its stunning eyes, which can be green, amber or gold, surrounded by dark and light rings of colour, give it a striking expression. Its soft, finely textured coat includes ruddy ('usual'), sorrel, chocolate, red and tortoiseshell colours.

Temperament

The Abyssinian is highly intelligent, inquisitive and affectionate. It has strong loyalty to its owner and likes to be involved in whatever is going on. Whilst maintaining an almost regal reserve, it can suddenly become incredibly playful. This breed enjoys company, but prefers not to be in larger pet groups.

Similar breeds

Abyssinian, Singapura, Sokoke, Somali

Size

Tom .... 3.5–4.5 kg/8–10 lb

Queen ... 2.5–3 kg/6–7 lb

Origin

The story goes that the first Abyssinian was a cat named 'Zula' brought to England from Abyssinia in 1862 by a British soldier. There is no clear link between Zula and modern Abyssinians and the breed is now thought to have originated in India. It was established in the UK by the mid-1890s and introduced to the USA in the early 1900s.

India

PERSIAN

TOM

The PERSIAN is one of the most iconic and easily recognizable breeds. With its lustrous fur, round face and big eyes, it's no wonder that it is seen as cuddly and teddy-bear like – the perfect pet cat, in fact. Variants of this breed have appeared on chocolate boxes and greetings cards for well over a century and the Persian has entered the human psyche as the epitome of the pedigree cat.

Features

A medium to large cat, with a cobby, well-muscled body and short legs, the Persian has a round, domed head and a 'flat' face that can be accentuated in some breeds as 'ultra type'. It has a small nose, large eyes and medium to small ears. Of course, the Persian's defining feature is its long coat, with a mane-like ruff surrounding its head and a thickly furred, plumed tail.

Temperament

This cat is slightly reserved at times but essentially calm and will show affection to its owners. It will mix well with children and other pets if it has to, but usually it prefers to be the focus of attention.

Similar breeds

Exotic Shorthair, Himalayan/Colourpoint Persian

Size

Tom .... 3.5–5 kg/8–11 lb

Queen ... 3–4 kg/7–9 lb

Origin

The first Persians were imported into Europe from Persia (Iran) in the seventeenth century and crossbred with Angoras. However, the modern breed is genetically grouped with other European breeds. It was first shown in 1871 in the UK. Persians were exported to the USA in the late nineteenth century and it is now an established, popular breed the world over.

UK

RUSSIAN BLUE (GCCF)

TOM

The Russian Blue is a short-haired, elegant cat with a distinctive gentle expression. It is one of the oldest show breeds, having first appeared in the UK in the 1860s and arriving in the USA in the early twentieth century. Most Russian Blues today are direct descendents of cats imported to the UK in the nineteenth century.

Features

Russian Blue breed standards vary across different associations – the UK's GCCF type has a short wedge, prominent whisker pads and large ears as well as an elegant body with a long tail and legs. Its short, thick coat is soft and silky in texture. Coat colour is medium blue, with an overall silvery sheen. The GCCF also recognizes Russian Whites and Russian Blacks.

Temperament

A highly intelligent, gentle and affectionate cat, the Russian Blue will form a strong bond with its owners. It has a tolerant nature and is quite happy to be handled, and it is patient with dogs and children and therefore an ideal family pet.

Similar breeds]

Nebelung, Russian Shorthair, Tiffanies

Size

Tom....... 4–6 kg/9–13 lb

Queen ... 3.5–5 kg/8–11 lb

Origin

Russian Blues were first known as Archangel cats, due to their place of origin, the Russian port of Arkhangelsk. The cats were introduced, via ship, to other European countries and formed part of the earliest roster of fancy breeds in the UK. The breed was shown at the UK's Crystal Palace cat show in 1875.

Russia

HIMALAYAN/COLOURPOINT PERSIAN
TOM

The HIMALAYAN/COLOURPOINT PERSIAN is a very attractive breed of cat, but is recognized in different ways by different cat registries – while TICA treats it as a separate breed to the Persian, the CFA classifies it as a division of the Persian breed and the GCCF calls it a Colourpoint Persian. It is, however, essentially a Persian cat, with attractive 'points' to its face, ears, tail and legs.

Features

This cat has a typical Persian physique: a cobby, fairly muscular body with short legs, a round, domed head, a snub nose and a 'flattened' face. It has small ears and large, round eyes, with a long, lustrous coat and brush-like tail. Its points are its most striking feature, and these come in a wide range of colours.

Temperament

This is an intelligent cat, affectionate towards its 'special human'. It has a calm disposition, although occasionally may be given to random bursts of mischief. It integrates well with human families and other pets. It isn't overly vocal, but has a very expressive face. This makes its feelings on a given matter very clear!

Similar breeds

Exotic Shorthair, Persian

Size

Tom .... 4–5.5 kg/9–12 lb

Queen ... 3–4 kg/7–9 lb

Origin

An experimental breeding programme to combine the traits of Persian and Siamese cats was undertaken in the 1930s at Harvard University, USA, while formal breeding programmes took place separately in the UK and USA in the early 1950s, both of which helped to produce the cat we see now.

USA

CORNISH REX

QUEEN

The CORNISH REX is a very distinctive breed of cat, with its long body covered in tightly curled down. Highly sought after by cat fanciers the world over, the Cornish Rex is also a firm favourite for pet cat owners as it integrates very well into family life. Alert, intelligent and totally handsome, the Cornish Rex knows it's a cut – or a wave at least – above the hoi poloi.

Features

This breed has a slender, lithe yet solid and muscular body, with a naturally arched back and tapering tail. A patrician, Roman nose, tall, high-set ears and oval eyes give it a very distinct expression. Of course, it is the downy fur, which falls in waves, either loose or tight, over the body, which stands out. Coat colour can vary from solid to tabby.

Temperament

This sociable cat thrives on being in the thick of the action! Highly intelligent and playful, affectionate and loyal, the Cornish Rex is the ideal family pet and mixes well with other pets. It tends to have a slightly higher body temperature than other breeds and enjoys lying in warm places.

Similar breeds

Devon Rex, LaPerm, Selkirk Rex, Siamese, Sphynx

Size

Tom .... 3.5–4.5 kg/8–10 lb

Queen ... 2.5–3 kg/5–7 lb

Origin

As its name suggests, the breed originated in Cornwall, UK. In 1950, a Siamese queen gave birth to a litter of five kittens, one of which had a distinctive curly coat, the first 'Rex'. Subsequent crosses with Siamese, Havanas and American and British Shorthairs fixed the Cornish Rex in the form it is now known.

UK

BIRMAN

TOM

The BIRMAN is perhaps best known for the Burmese legend, in which a beautiful white cat stood watch while the high priest died. Upon the priest's death, his soul transferred to the cat, whereupon its coat turned brown and cream while its paws and hocks, where it had sat on the priest's chest, remained white. The cat looked up at the priest's golden goddess and its eyes turned as sapphire blue as hers.

Features

This lovely, medium-sized longhaired cat is cream coloured, with points coming in a range of colours. All four feet are white with laces halfway up the back legs. The Birman's face is round and features a Roman nose. It has stunning, rather round, sapphire blue eyes and a soft, chirping voice.

Temperament

Very sweet natured, a Birman gets along well with other pets and with children but can also live as an only pet. Gentle and patient, but playful, it is a wonderful companion that enjoys participating in whatever its owner is doing. A Birman can become 'verbal' if its owner talks to it.

Similar breed

Ragdoll

Size

Tom .... 3.5–5.5 kg/8–12 lb

Queen ... 3–4 kg/7–9 lb

Origin

The Birman was originally from Burma. Although it is unknown when it was first exported, it was first recognized in France in the 1920s and the UK and USA in the 1960s. Most Birmans can be traced to France, the UK, Australia and Germany although genetically it is grouped with other Southeast Asian breeds.

Burma

DEVON REX
TOM

With its curly fur, high cheekbones and pointed ears, it is little wonder that the DEVON REX is often referred to as 'The Pixie Cat', or, for the more sci-fi aware of cat lovers, as 'The Alien Cat'. Although the Devon Rex and the Cornish Rex were first discovered in adjacent counties in the UK, genetically the two breeds are completely different.

Features

The Devon Rex has a slightly wedge-shaped head, prominent cheekbones and a compact muzzle. It has large, low set ears and wide, expressive eyes, which add to its pixie-like features. Its small- to medium-sized compact body is covered with the soft, curly coat that is its defining feature. Its hind legs are longer than its forelegs, which does hinder its ability to play, climb and jump.

Temperament

With behaviour best described as 'impish', this mischievous and intelligent cat is fond of exploring and climbing into inaccessible places. It enjoys snuggling on its favourite human's shoulder, nuzzling close. Needless to say, the Devon is a great family pet.

Similar breeds

Cornish Rex, LaPerm, Selkirk Rex, Sphynx

Size

Tom.......3.5–4 kg/8–9 lb

Queen...2.5–3 kg/6–7 lb

Origin

The breed originated in the 1960s from a curly haired feral tom that lived near an abandoned tin mine in Devon, UK. It sired a litter to a domestic female, of which one was a curly haired kitten named Kirlee.

UK

BOMBAY

TOM

While at first glance of a BOMBAY cat, you're liable to wonder how a small panther has appeared in civilization, there is absolutely no wildcat breed behind it. There are actually two different Bombay breeds – the American Bombay and the British Bombay – though both are striking, solid black cats related to the Burmese.

Features

This unforgettable feline is sleek and muscular at the same time while wrapped in a coat of the deepest, darkest black, with golden or copper eyes (the British Bombay can also have green eyes). Its shiny, tight black coat does little shedding and requires minimal care. A medium-sized cat, its muscles make it heavier than it appears.

Temperament

The Bombay loves other pets when properly introduced. It can be leash-trained and does well with well-mannered children. Mischievous, intelligent and playful, this cat will want to be a part of whatever is happening in the house, acting as a four-legged assistant. And when you sit down, this sweet, loving and people-oriented cat will happily settle into your lap.

Similar breeds

American Shorthair, British Shorthair, Burmese

Size

Tom .... 3.5–5 kg/8–11 lb

Queen ... 2.5–4 kg/6–9 lb

Origin

The American Bombay was created by Nikki Horner of Louisville, Kentucky, who began developing the breed in the 1950s by crossing the black American Shorthair and the sable Burmese. The British Bombay is a slightly more recent breed and is a result of mating a Burmese with a British Shorthair.

USA, UK

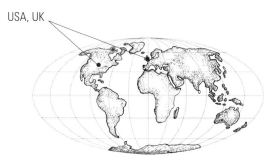

BRITISH SHORTHAIR

QUEEN

The British Shorthair, colloquially known as the 'teddy bear cat', is one of the UK's oldest cat breeds and one of the oldest breeds of the Cat Fancy. It is said that it hasn't changed much since it first arrived with the Roman invasion. Once known as an excellent mouser, this sweet cat now probably spends more time hunting for a toy than any prey.

Features

With its large, round eyes and smiling face, complete with round cheeks, it's no wonder that the British Shorthair was allegedly the model for the Cheshire Cat in Lewis Carroll's *Alice in Wonderland*. This cat is sturdy, with a dense, thick coat. It can come in a wide range of coat colours, although blue is the most popular.

Temperament

A British Shorthair will get along with other pets and has been known to live happily with dogs, birds and rabbits. It prefers to have its feet on the ground but it's content to sit next to its owner. It can be clumsy and have occasional bursts of kittenish energy as an adult.

Similar breeds

British Longhair, Chartreux

Size

Tom .... 4–7.5 kg/9–17 lb

Queen ... 3–5.5 kg/7–12 lb

Origin

Despite the breed's name, the British Shorthair originated in Egypt, arriving in England alongside the Roman invaders, where it found a home and a name in its new country. It was recognised by TICA in 1979 and the CFA in 1980, but it is still quite rare in the USA.

Egypt

SIBERIAN

T O M

The SIBERIAN is a very old Russian breed dating back hundreds of years, and it has featured in fairytales and children's books from the 1800s. Originally a working farm cat, the Siberian is considered a Russian national treasure and, for all of its size and power, is an extremely gentle soul. Intelligent enough to problem solve, and playful, it is also adept at comforting those who need it.

Features

This breed reaches it full, impressive size at five years old. It has big paws, slightly longer back legs and amazing agility. A semi-longhair, it has a triple coat for the Russian winter – this is then shed. Siberians come in a range of coat colours, with striking eyes that are gold to green. Some people consider this cat hypo-allergenic.

Temperament

A sweet, calm, loving cat that wants to be near its owners, a Siberian likes children, dogs and other animals and all manner of toys and games. It clowns about, is partial to jumping or climbing quite high and communicates in soft trills.

Similar breed

Maine Coon, Norwegian Forest Cat, Turkish Van

Size

Tom .... 5.5–8 kg/12–18 lb

Queen ... 4–6.5 kg/9–14 lb

Origin

Prior to the 1800s, there is little documented evidence of this cat's earliest history in Russia. Although it was recorded that Siberians were shown in 1871 in the UK and in 1884 in the USA, the breed as it is recognized today was first imported into the USA in 1990 and the UK in 2002.

Russia

NEBELUNG

TOM

The Nebelung is a relatively new breed and still quite rare. It was created to look like the longhaired cats seen in Russia in the early nineteenth century that were then imported to England. It loves its people but will probably disappear when strangers arrive. Its long blue coat is frosted with silver, giving an ethereal appearance to this intelligent and playful cat.

Features

This medium-sized cat with large ears has been described as both longhaired and medium coated. Its coat is silky to the touch and it has wide-set eyes that can range anywhere from yellowish green to green in colour. The Nebulung is sturdy and well muscled.

Temperament

Playful and active, this sweet, loving and intelligent breed of cat loves to sit on its owner's lap, and will follow its person from room to room. However, it is essentially shy with strangers and young children and takes time to adjust to new owners and family members.

Similar breed

Havana Brown, Russian Blue, Russian Shorthair

Size

Tom .... 3.5–5 kg/8–11 lb

Queen ... 2.5–4 kg/6–9 lb

Origin

The Russian Blue was the designated outcross for this breed, which was created in the USA in 1986 from two cats named Brunhilde and Siegfried. The breed was recognized by TICA the following year and granted preliminary recognition by GCCF in 2012.

USA

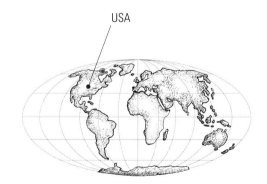

TONKINESE

TOM

The Tonkinese, one of the most captivating of cats with its amazing aqua eyes and beautiful coat, is actually one of the breeds which feature in the *Tamra Maew* manuscripts (Thai cat poems written during the Ayudhya Period, 1351–1767). A cross between the Siamese and the Burmese, you simply cannot ignore this gorgeous and good-natured cat.

Features

The first breed with aqua eyes, the Tonk has a short, muscular body with a soft, luxurious coat almost like mink. This coat comes in a dozen colours and pattern varieties, including pointed, mink and solid varieties; cats in the solid coat colour are the only ones to have green to yellow-green eyes.

Temperament

Gregarious and fun loving, a Tonkinese is likely to help greet guests at the door. It is a sweet cat that enjoys discussing the day's events and loves to play. It is quite capable of inventing its own games and, with its ability to be a lap cat, the Tonkinese can be all things to its lucky owner.

Similar breeds

Bengal, Burmese, Korat, Khao Manee, Siamese

Size

Tom .... 3.5–5.5 kg/8–12 lb

Queen ... 2.5–3.5 kg/6–8 lb

Origin

The Tonkinese first appeared in the UK in the early nineteenth century. The first Tonkinese cat to be exported to the USA, in 1930, was Wong Mau, originally thought to be a Burmese. The modern Tonkinese was developed from outcrossing Siamese and Burmese in Canada.

Thailand

SOKOKE

TOM

The Sokoke, native to Kenya, is so old that there are no records of when the breed began. The Giriama, one of the Nyika tribes of the coastal region of Kenya, were the first people to discover and live with these cats. This rare breed loves its family members, both human and feline alike, and is a devoted companion.

Features

Graceful, medium-sized and muscular, the Sokoke has a ticked, modified, classic tabby coat – the distinctive pattern and colouring can actually make it look transparent from a distance.

Temperament

The Sokoke is described as intelligent, curious, sensitive, interactive, intuitive and peace-loving. It is a moderately active and territorial breed that is well aware of any family hierarchy, not only of pets but of people as well. This cat enjoys being with its owners and as a kitten can create its own games and play for hours on its own.

Similar breed

Abyssinian, Singapura, Somali

Size

Tom........5–6.5 kg/11–14 lb

Queen...3.5–5 kg/8–11 lb

Origin

The Sokoke is bred from feral, wild cats native to Kenya. Known as the Old Line, a set of these cats were imported to Denmark and Italy in the 1980s and 1990s. The New Line also originates in Kenya, and a set of these cats were imported to the USA in the early 2000s to improve the Old Line's bloodline.

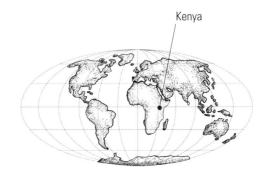

Kenya

CYMRIC

TOM

The Cymric – tailless or possessing a vestigial stump where its tail should be – is a semi-longhaired breed derived from the Manx. Some cat registries consider the Cymric simply to be a Semi-Longhaired Manx, whilst others recognize it as a separate breed. The name 'Cymric' is in recognition of the Manx's possible Welsh origins – 'Cymru' being Welsh for Wales.

Features

This medium-sized cat has a cobby, well-rounded but muscular body, with well-spaced ears and round eyes. Like the Manx, its hind legs are longer than its forelegs, which causes its tailless rump to sit higher than usual, producing an arched appearance. Its coat is medium length and quite dense. The Cymric can be theoretically bred in all colours and patterns, although recognition of these differs between cat registries.

Temperament

An intelligent, curious cat with a gentle disposition, the Cymric is very loyal to its owners and enjoys company, although it does not demand attention. It is playful and enjoys climbing, and it mixes well with other pets.

Similar breeds

Japanese Bobtail, Karelian Bobtail, Kurilian Bobtail, Manx

Size

Tom .... 4.5–5.5 kg/10–12 lb

Queen ... 3.5–4.5 kg/8–10 lb

Origin

Cymrics originated in the Isle of Man, though breeders there tried to avoid intentionally breeding kittens with the longhaired gene. However, in Canada during the 1960s, some breeders bred longhaired Manxes with the aim of producing a new breed. This was to eventually be known as the Cymric.

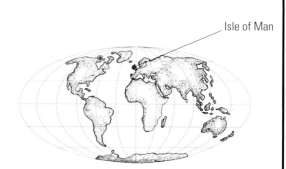

Isle of Man

SINGAPURA
QUEEN

The SINGAPURA is mischief itself, with a lot of personality in a small package. Recognized as a living national treasure in 1991 by the Singaporean government, its ticked coat pattern and dark brown colour is native to Southeast Asia. This cat is usually found on the highest perch possible and will like riding on your shoulder where it's off the ground and can 'help' you with whatever you're doing.

Features

This little imp, the smallest of all cats, comes in only one colour, sable brown ticking on an ivory background, which often has yellow tones and fades underneath. Its capivating eyes are celadon green, hazel, gold or copper.

Temperament

A playful and lively cat known for its intelligence, the Singapura has a desire to interact with its people. Adventurous even in old age, it will only curl up on your lap when it's ready for a cuddle or a nap. Its personality will captivate you and life will never be dull but it might be exhausting if you don't channel some of that energy into positive training.

Similar breeds

Abyssinian, Sokoke, Somali

Size

Tom .... 2.5–3.5 kg/6–8 lb

Queen ... 2–2.5 kg/5–6 lb

Origin

Though there is some controversy over the Singapura's origins, it appears that the breed was developed in the USA from three street cats native to Singapore that were imported in the 1970s by Hal and Tommy Meadows. The breed was introduced to the UK in 1988.

Singapore

EXOTIC SHORTHAIR

TOM

The EXOTIC SHORTHAIR is essentially a shorthaired Persian – or at least a cat of the typical Persian body type with short, dense fur. The breed was developed separately on both sides of the Atlantic and has gone on to gain great popularity. It is the ideal cat for those who love the Persian's 'look' but can't be bothered to spend a lot of time grooming its fur!

Features

This breed has a medium-sized, cobby but muscular body, a round head with the typical Persian 'flattened' face, a small, snub nose, ears rounded at the tips and large, round eyes. Its fur is thicker than an ordinary shorthaired cat, rather more fluffy and dense. It is bred in a vast range of colours and patterns, including blue, black, lilac, red, tabby, tortoiseshell and pointed in Persian colours.

Temperament

A gentle, curious cat, the Exotic Shorthair is somewhat less reserved than its Persian ancestors. It is very affectionate and will follow its owner around the house in a dog-like manner. It is playful and outgoing, mixing well with other cats and pets.

Similar breeds

Himalayan/Colourpoint Persian, Persian

Size

Tom .... 4.5–6.5 kg/10–14 lb

Queen ... 3–4.5 kg/7–10 lb

Origin

The breed was developed originally in the USA in the 1970s by crossing Persians with American Shorthairs. A similar development programme was started in the UK in the early 1980s by crossing Persians and British Shorthairs.

USA

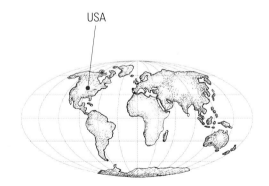

OCICAT
QUEEN

The Ocicat does resemble the small wildcat Ocelot species. However, it has no more of a wild or feral genetic background than any other domesticated breed and it is certainly not related to the Ocelot. The Ocicat was created from mating Siamese and Abyssinian cats, with additional mating to American Shorthairs.

Features

The Ocicat has a strong, large body and muscular legs. Its head is wedge shaped, strong jawed, with large ears, rounded at the tips, and almond-shaped eyes ringed with darker fur. Its coat is short and dense, marked with dark contrasting spots. It is bred in varying colours, including tawny, cinnamon, chocolate and fawn, with the same colour variants in silver. Ocicats with a striped rather than spotted coat pattern are known as Ocicat Classics.

Temperament

This breed is extrovert and quite dog-like in its devotion to its owner. Indeed, Ocicats enjoy playing with toys and will play fetch. Its gregarious nature makes it an ideal family pet and it will mix well with other pets as long as they realize that the Ocicat is the boss!

Similar breeds

Abyssinian, American Shorthair, Ocicat, Siamese

Size

Tom .... 4–6.5 kg/9–14 lb

Queen ... 2.5–4 kg/6–9 lb

Origin

Created in the USA in the 1960s from a mating of a Siamese and an Abyssinian, the breed's distinctive markings didn't appear until the second generation, in the form of a spotted kitten nicknamed 'Ocicat'.

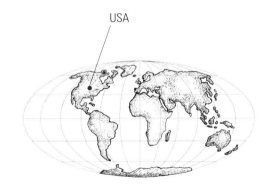

USA

LAPERM

TOM

From 1980s American barn cat rex mutation to esteemed show-ring cat today, the striking, curly haired LaPerm has managed to captivate its audience and acquire an active, international group of admirers since its first exhibition.

Features

The LaPerm's soft coat ranges from wavy to curly, with tighter curls to be found underneath the chin and on the tummy. The coat has been called 'The Gypsy Shag' and it comes in every conceivable colour and pattern.

Temperament

This active cat is intelligent, curious and can be fairly easily trained to do any number of tricks. Content also to sit on laps and purr, it loves people as much as people love running their fingers through its curly coat. A LaPerm will enjoy following its owner around, even riding on a shoulder. One way or another, this cat will be with its person.

Similar breed

Cornish Rex, Devon Rex, Selkirk Rex, Sphynx

Size

Tom....... 3.5–4.5 kg/8–10 lb

Queen ... 2.5–3.5 kg/6–8 lb

Origin

This breed has its origins in Oregon, USA, where one of Linda Koehl's brown tabby barn cats gave birth to a hairless kitten; the short, sparse, curly coat that emerged at six weeks was a rex mutation. By the 1990s, Linda had started a breeding program for the 'LaPerm', named in honour of its coat.

USA

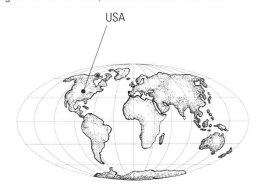

RUSSIAN BLUE (TICA)

TOM

The RUSSIAN BLUE was imported into the USA in the early 1900s and eventually established itself as a very popular breed among emergent cat fanciers. With its regal bearing and aristocratic expression, it's easy to see why this cat was beloved of the tzars in its native Russia.

Features

Russian Blue breed standards vary across different associations – the TICA standard calls for a medium-sized cat with a 'foreign' type, lithe and muscular body. The wedge-shaped head, with its distinctive, alluring smile, has seven angular plains, high cheekbones and large flared ears. The coat is short, dense and blue overall, no other colour variant being recognized.

Temperament

The Russian Blue is an intelligent and it can form a close bond with its owner. This cat mixes well with other pets and it is very affectionate with children, making it an ideal family pet.

Similar breeds

Havana Brown, Nebelung, Russian Shorthair

Size

Tom.......4.5–7 kg/10–15 lb

Queen...3.5–7 kg/8–15 lb

Origin

Although the Russian Blue was introduced to the USA in the early twentieth century, serious breeding didn't take off until after World War II, when American breeders imported both Scandinavian and British cats in order to combine the best features of each.

Russia

BURMILLA
QUEEN

The Burmilla is the happy outcome of accidentally pairing a newly acquired Chinchilla Persian with an escaped lilac Burmese – the four female shorthaired silver kittens with black shading were so beautiful that their owners decided to begin a breeding programme for them. This breed's gorgeous silver coat and bedazzling green eyes are certainly a sight to behold.

Features

Elegant, yet muscular, the adult Burmilla has a sparkling silver coat and green eyes that range from yellowish green to gold when it's young. This cat has what seems to be 'make-up' lining its eyes, nose and lips, making it appear all the more striking. It comes in two coat varieties: shorthaired and semi-longhaired.

Temperament

The sweet Burmilla can be independent but loves its owner and can manage to act like a kitten even when older. This cat can be as impish as a Burmese and as relaxed as a Chinchilla Persian. It loves to play and gets along with other pets in the family as well as children.

Similar breeds

Burmese, Chinchilla Persian, Tiffanie

Size

Tom.......4.5–5.5 kg/10–12 lb

Queen...3.5–4.5 kg/8–10 lb

Origin

This new breed began life in the UK, from the accidental mating of a Chinchilla Persian and a lilac Burmese. One of the newer breeds to gain recognition by the cat registries, it is fairly hard to find in the USA.

UK

AUSTRALIAN MIST

TOM

The AUSTRALIAN MIST is still a relatively rare breed outside of its native Australia, but these delightful spotted cats – well named for their delicate, almost mist-like coat colouration – give every indication of one day becoming as well known as British and American Shorthairs.

Features

This medium-sized, shorthaired cat has a round head that is delicately marked with bars of colour, medium-sized ears and expressive, round eyes. It has a short coat, with no undercoat, and its spotted coat patterns and base colour appear as though veiled, giving an overall 'misty' effect. The Australian Mist's legs and tail are marked with rings or bars and it is bred in brown, blue, chocolate, lilac, gold and peach.

Temperament

The Australian Mist is a calm, loving cat that thrives on human contact and prefers to stay close to home. Very people-fixated and gregarious, this playful Antipodean feline mixes well with other cats and pets, making it an ideal family pet.

Similar breeds

Abyssinian, American Shorthair, British Shorthair, Burmese

Size

Tom .... 4.5–6 kg/10–13 lb

Queen ... 3.5–4.5 kg/8–10 lb

Origin

The breed was developed in Australia in the mid-1970s by crossing Burmese, Abyssinian and various domestic shorthaired cats. The first Australian Mists were exported to the UK and USA in the early years of the twenty-first century.

Australia

CHARTREUX

TOM

The CHARTREUX, known as 'the smiling blue cat of France', is an ancient, natural breed renowned for its hunting prowess. There are two competing legends for its name: some believe the cats lived among French Carthusian Monks, makers of the famous Charteuse liqueur; while others claim the name relates to an eighteenth-century Spanish wool similar to the breed's dense coat.

Features

One of only three Blue breeds, this cat has rounded eyes that range from gold to copper, with a softly contoured forehead and round head that gently tapers to a narrowed muzzle. The Chartreux has a double coat – a more waterproof outer coat and a wooly undercoat – and its robust body and fine-boned legs have often led to descriptions of it being 'a potato on toothpicks'.

Temperament

Very intelligent, this cat enjoys playing fetch and watching birds and television. This sweet, calm cat has a soft chirping voice and tends to follow its people around, sitting next to, rather than on, them. Very stable, it prefers to have its feet on the ground.

Similar breeds

British Shorthair, British Longhair, Persian

Size

Tom .... 4.5–6.5 kg/10–14 lb

Queen ... 2.5–4 kg/6–9 lb

Origin

Probably originating in the Middle East and arriving in France during the Crusades, this natural breed has been noted in French documents since the sixteenth century. The breed suffered during World War II, after which other breeds, most notably the Persian and the British Shorthair, were introduced.

Middle East

MANX
QUEEN

One fanciful story about the origins of the Manx is that Noah accidentally cut its tail off when he closed the Ark door. In fact, this cat is a genetic mutation that started within the feline population on the Isle of Man, hence its name, Manx. Kittens born with this mutation were known as either 'rumpies' – with no tail at all – or 'stumpies' – with a small vestige of a tail.

Features

A medium-sized cat with very rounded features, the Manx is broadchested and firmly muscled with a round head, wide, round eyes and strong legs. Its hind legs are longer than its forelegs, causing its rump to be higher than the shoulder. This, together with the lack of a full tail, gives the cat an overall rounded outline. It can be bred in virtually every coat colour and pattern.

Temperament

The Manx is a calm, even-tempered, intelligent cat. It is very people-orientated, forming a strong bond with its people. It is playful and can be quite vocal, demanding attention in its unique, trilling voice. It will mix well with other pets.

Similar breeds

Cymric, Japanese Bobtail, Karelian Bobtail, Kurilian Bobtail

Size

Tom .... 4.5–5.5 kg/10–12 lb

Queen ... 3.5–4.5 kg/8–10 lb

Origin

The Manx originated several hundred years ago thanks to a spontaneous genetic mutation among the cats on the Isle of Man. While it is unknown when the cat was first imported into the USA, it was one of the founding breeds when the CFA was created in 1906.

Isle of Man

ORIENTAL SHORTHAIR
TOM

The ORIENTAL SHORTHAIR is derived from the Siamese, and from matings with Abyssinian, British Shorthair and Russian Blue cats. The result is a lively and intelligent cat with the lithe, graceful body contours of the Siamese and similar Oriental-type breeds but with a greater range of coat colours and patterns.

Features

This cat has a long, slender body, and is well muscled with long legs and a whip-like tail. It has a wedge-shaped head, topped off with large, erect ears and striking almond-shaped eyes. Its coat is short and sleek, whilst its Oriental Longhaired relative has semi-long fur. Both are bred in solid colours, which include cream, red, brown, lilac and ebony, and various coat patterns including tabby, bi-colour, smoke and shaded.

Temperament

This breed is intelligent, inquisitive and very sociable. It enjoys human company and will mix well with other animals, making it an ideal family pet. It is very energetic and playful and needs to engage its formidable brain as much as its body.

Similar breeds

Abyssinian, British Shorthair, Russian Blue, Siamese

Size

Tom.......5–6.5 kg/11–14 lb

Queen...4–5.5 kg/9–12 lb

Origin

This breed was created in the 1950s in the UK, from matings between Abyssinians, Siamese, British Shorthairs and Russian Blues. They were imported into the USA in the 1970s and rapidly grew in popularity.

UK

KHAO MANEE

TOM

The KHAO MANEE may be a new breed as far as the Western Cat Fancy is concerned, but it is in fact one of the four ancient Thai breeds (the others being the Siamese, Burmese and Korat). It is mentioned in *Tamra Maew* manuscripts. Khao Manee translated means 'White Gem', which sums up this graceful, pure white breed perfectly.

Features

The Khao Manee is a small- to medium-sized cat, with a typical 'foreign' body type: lithe and muscular with a tail as long as the body. It has a heart-shaped head with high cheekbones. One of its most notable features is its odd-coloured eyes – usually one blue and one amber, although this can vary. It has a shining white coat, made up of short, close-lying fur.

Temperament

This extremely intelligent cat has an outgoing, friendly personality. It will play vigorously or lie on its owner's lap contentedly in equal measure. If a Khao Manee thinks it's not getting enough attention, it will simply jump on to your shoulder and tell you it's there!

Similar breeds

Bengal, Burmese, Korat, Siamese, Tonkinese

Size

Tom .... 4–5 kg/9–11 lb

Queen ... 3–3.5 kg/7–8 lb

Origin

The Khao Manee is an ancient Thai breed which was greatly favored by Thai royalty. It wasn't until 1999 that the first Khao Manees were imported into the USA, with further offspring imported to the UK ten years later.

Thailand

SIAMESE

QUEEN

Stunning looks, natural grace and a distinctive range of colourations make the SIAMESE instantly recognizable. With a regal visage that evokes visions of Asian palaces and cats living in the lap of luxury as feline gods, this keenly intelligent cat was dubbed 'The Royal Cat of Siam' when first exported to the West in the late 1800s.

Features

The Siamese has a slim, well-muscled body with short, fine, sleek fur. It has a wedge-shaped head, with deep blue, almond-shaped eyes and large ears. Its legs are long and elegant, its tail slender. The Siamese is a pointed cat, the extremities of the body being coloured, whilst the main body is white or shaded. The classic Siamese is seal point, although many different variations exist.

Temperament

The Siamese is a very intelligent and affectionate breed which bonds closely with its owners. It has a playful personality and displays dog-like behavior. A Siamese will enjoy being involved in anything of interest! It has a very distinct, loud voice, often mistaken for a baby crying.

Similar breeds

Bengal, Burmese, Korat, Khao Manee, Tonkinese

Size

Tom.......4.5–7 kg/10–15 lb

Queen...3.5–5.5 kg/8–12 lb

Origin

The Siamese originated in Thailand, formerly Siam, although cats of a similar type are shown in ancient Egyptian illustrations. The first Siamese exported from Thailand to the USA may have been a gift from an American diplomat in Bangkok to First Lady Lucy Hayes in 1879. Siamese were first bred in the UK in 1884.

Thailand

SOMALI

TOM

The Somali is a stunning cat. With its striking ruddy colouration, large ears and bushy tail, it's little wonder that this breed is sometimes known as the 'Fox Cat'. It is derived from the Abyssinian, a breed with which it shares many traits. It is a cat possessed of a great curiosity and energy, and this makes it an ideal family pet – if it can sit still long enough!

Features

The Somali is a well-muscled, medium-sized cat, with a silky, semi-longhaired coat. Its head is medium wedge shape, with large ears and almond-shaped eyes that vary in colour from green to copper. The body is set off with a magnificent fluffy tail. The 'usual' Somali coat is golden brown ticked with black, although it is also bred in a variety of colours, including sorrel (red), silver, blue silver, cream lilac, tabby and various tortie points.

Temperament

Highly intelligent and inquisitive, the Somali is very energetic, loves human company and will show great loyalty to its owner. Generally speaking, this breed doesn't like large cat populations where it has to compete for attention.

Similar breed

Singapura, Sokoke, Somali

Size

Tom .... 3.5–4.5 kg/8–10 lb

Queen ... 2.5–3 kg/6–7 lb

Origin

The Somali originated from longhaired Abyssinian kittens born in the UK in the 1940s then exported to the USA, Canada, Australia and New Zealand. In the 1960s the breed was developed independently in each country. The Somali's name is simply due to the fact that Somalia borders Ethiopia, formerly Abyssinia.

UK

SNOWSHOE

QUEEN

The SNOWSHOE is a relatively rare breed. Bred out of the Siamese and American Shorthair, it is a 'pointed' cat with a longish, but muscular body. The cat's name is derived from its distinctive white paws, which look as though it has walked through snow. Highly intelligent, it is one of the very few breeds that actively likes to play in water!

Features

Described as 'deceptively powerful', the Snowshoe has strong musculature. Its head shape is similar to the 'applehead' of the 'old type' Siamese. It has a short- to medium-length coat, and can be bred in a range of solid colours, with dark points to its face, tail and ears and sometimes its legs. It will always have blue eyes and white feet.

Temperament

Intelligent and with an extrovert personality, this cat enjoys playing with toys, climbing and generally making its presence known. It has a distinctive voice, softer than a Siamese. The Snowshoe is fond of playing with running water and enjoys both human and animal company.

Similar breeds

Ragdoll, Siamese

Size

Tom .... 4–5.5 kg/9–12 lb

Queen ... 3–4.5 kg/7–10 lb

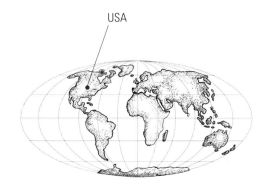

Origin

The breed originated in the USA in the 1960s when a litter of Siamese kittens was born with white feet. These were later crossed to bicolour American Shorthairs, producing the cat we recognize as the Snowshoe today.

USA

KORAT
QUEEN

The Korat is an ancient breed from Siam – present-day Thailand – where it is called the 'Si-Sawat'. It is one of the seventeen Good Luck Cats to appear in the *Tamra Maew* manuscripts. Despite its long history, it is possibly the cat that has most retained its original look and, unsurprisingly, it is considered a symbol of good fortune.

Features

This breed's short, single, silver-tipped blue coat and Peridot green eyes create a striking visual effect, while its somewhat cobby, small- to medium-sized body is comprised of four 'heart' shapes, seen by looking at the cat from various perspectives. Muscular and powerful, the Korat is more solid than it appears, with amazing hearing, sight and smell.

Temperament

A Korat is quite capable of chirping and even roaring but you won't hear much from it unless it needs to tell you something. Intelligent, athletic and gentle with children, it prefers a quiet household. A Korat loves to cuddle and sit as closely as possible to its owners.

Similar breeds

Bengal, Burmese, Khao Manee, Siamese, Tonkinese

Size

Tom .... 3.5–4.5 kg/8–10 lb

Queen ... 2.5–3.5 kg/6–8 lb

Origin

The Korat is an ancient breed from Siam. The breed may have been shown in England in the late 1800s under the misnomer of 'Siamese'. The first Korats were imported into the USA in the late 1950s and all cats imported since then can trace their ancestry back to Thailand.

Thailand

TIFFANIE
QUEEN

The TIFFANIE, a rare jewel of a cat that is slowly gaining popularity, is a semi-longhaired breed that is part of the 'Asian' group of varieties, sometimes known by the name of Asian Semi-Longhair. It is recognized by the GCCF in the UK, but not the main USA cat registries (there is a totally unrelated American breed known as 'Tiffany' or 'Chantilly').

Features

The Tiffanie is a medium- to large-sized cat of compact build, similar to its Burmese ancestors, with a firm musculature. It has wide-set ears, round, expressive eyes of varying colour and an alert expression. Its fur is semi-longhaired and fine, including a plume-like tail. The Tiffanie can be bred in a wide range of colours and patterns, including black, chocolate, cinnamon, red, lilac, fawn, tabby, shaded and tortie.

Temperament

The Tiffanie loves to play and get involved in anything of interest but also likes nothing better than to cuddle up on its owner's lap. It is intelligent but quite possessive of its owner and doesn't generally mix very well with other pets.

Similar breeds

Burmese, Burmilla, Chinchilla Persian

Size

Tom.......4.5–7 kg/10–15 lb

Queen...3.5–4.5 kg/8–10 lb

Origin

The Asian group of cats was created in the UK due to an accidental mating between a Chinchilla Persian male and a Burmese female, resulting in the first Burmilla kittens. The longhaired gene inherited from the Chinchilla Persian arose in later Burmillas to give rise to the Tiffanie.

UK

NORWEGIAN FOREST CAT
TOM

The Norwegian Forest Cat, or Wegie, is thought to be the cat the Vikings took with them to keep their ships rodent-free. Some may have arrived on North America's east coast with Leif Erickson or someone of that time during the late tenth century. This sweet-natured cat has been named by King Olaf as the official cat of Norway, where it is called *Skagkott*, or 'Forest Cat'.

Features

The Wegie is large and muscular with a semi-longhaired double coat that has a thick undercoat as well as a bushy tail and tufted paws, all to keep it warm in its native Norwegian climate. This cat's water-resistant coat comes in most colours and becomes thicker in winter, as does its ruff. Its large, almond-shaped eyes and equilateral, triangle-shaped head give it a striking appearance.

Temperament

The Norwegian Forest Cat does very well indoors even though it's semi-active. A very sweet breed, it loves people and pets alike and will be sure to spend time with its owner, sharing games during its brief bursts of energy and sitting on laps when it suits.

Similar breeds

Maine Coon, Siberian, Turkish Van

Size

Tom.......5.5–7.5 kg/12–16 lb

Queen...4–5.5 kg/9–12 lb

Origin

This natural breed has featured in Norwegian mythology and folk tales for centuries. The breed may have become extinct if not for Norway's special preservation programme started in the 1970s. The breed was first exported to various European countries during the 1970s, then to the USA in 1979 and to the UK in 1987.

Norway

BURMESE
QUEEN

Thanks to its huge personality and striking looks, the playful and bright BURMESE is popular all around the world as both a pet and show animal. It is one of the four breeds to originate in Thailand (the others are the Siamese, Korat and Khao Manee). Its Thai name – 'Suphalak' – translates as 'beautiful appearance', which is very appropriate for this regal feline.

Features

The Burmese on both sides of the Atlantic is medium sized, with a surprisingly heavy muscle build. The American-type Burmese has a cobby body and rounded features, whilst the UK-type has a more triangular, 'Oriental-type' face. Both have large, lustrous eyes and shading to face, ears, legs and tail. This cat has a short, silky coat, the original colour of which is brown, but it is available in other colours, depending on the cat registry.

Temperament

This breed is very sociable and likes to be involved in everything that's going on. Curiosity is a very prominent feature, so a Burmese's owner can fully expect to have every nook and cranny of the house carefully explored!

Similar breeds

Korat, Siamese, Singapura, Tonkinese

Size

Tom .... 4–5.5 kg/9–12 lb

Queen ... 3.5–4.5 kg/8–10 lb

Origin

The modern Burmese was originally introduced to the USA from Thailand in 1930 via a single female cat which was then crossed with a Siamese. In the UK the breed officially began with a pair of Burmese imported from Thailand in 1949.

Thailand

SPHYNX
QUEEN

The Sphynx is a hairless cat that, with its wrinkled, wizened face, was so named because it also resembles the Egyptian Sphinx of Giza. This loving cat is the result of a recessive hairlessness gene, first seen in the 1960s in a kitten named Prune. This cat may need a wardrobe of sweaters for cold weather and will often sleep under its owner's blankets at night.

Features

A Sphynx does have some fine hair on its body and some even have discernable hair. Described as feeling like a peach, a warm hot water bottle or a chamois, the skin of a Sphynx is often oily, requiring skincare, and it usually requires weekly baths. It is a medium-sized cat, but not delicate.

Temperament

Friendly, lively and inquisitive, this breed gets along with cats and dogs alike. A Sphynx has been known to wrap its arms around its owner's neck and deliver kisses. It enjoys greeting visitors and will often appear clumsy in a bid for attention. Interestingly, it will use its toes like fingers while checking out something new.

Similar breeds

Cornish Rex, Devon Rex, LaPerm, Selkirk Rex

Size

Tom.......3.5–5 kg/8–11 lb

Queen...2.5–3.5/6–8 lb

Origin

The first hairless kitten appeared in the 1960s, the offspring of a black and white cat, in Ontario, Canada. After much experimentation, by the 1970s, hairless kittens were seen as natural mutations in several parts of North America. Since then they have been bred around the world.

Canada

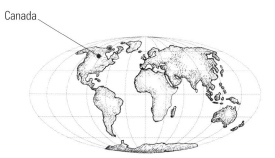

REPORTAGE

All you CAT FANCIERS, prepare to enjoy a rare and privileged CAT'S EYE VIEW and a behind-the-bench-curtains peek at what *getting ready for show time* is like for THE TALENT at a cat show. For those who have always wanted to know what their PURRING PETS are really thinking, now's your chance to find out. It's *cat-talk on the catwalk time!*

The Supreme
Cat Show,
NEC,
Birmingham, UK

Yes, I did wash
behind my ears

I'll show my face
when I'm ready

My teeth are a cut above yours

Handle with care

We all need a catnap today

Oh, the indignity!

There's a claws in my contract about this

teeth, check;
ears, check;
general health, check;
breed standard, check

TICA in Bloom, Oxford, UK

How cute am I?

We're all feline at our best today!

May the best cat win!

Check out my
'over the shoulder' look

There's a furry good chance
I'll win this

Everyone's a winner

I am going to get my paws on that rosette

I'm purr-fect

I am the cat's whiskers

We're all winning pawsibilities

I'm head and tail above the rest

Best in Show

GLOSSARY

All Breed Show A show open to all recognized breeds of pedigree cat at which the cats will be judged against each other.

Any Other Colour (AOC) A class for cats with coat colours not previously covered in a show's schedule.

Any Other Variety (AOV) A class for all cat breeds not previously covered in a show's schedule, sometimes including breeds that are not eligible to compete for titles.

Bloodline A group of related cats from a particular lineage.

Breed standard The ideal characteristics and judging criteria for the breed, as agreed upon by breeders and registries.

Breeder The breeder of a cat is technically the owner of the cat's dam (mother) at the time of mating.

Calling The characteristic vocalizations made by a female cat when in heat.

Cat Fancy The term given to the national or international group of individuals, clubs and registering associations involved with the breeding and showing of cats.

Cattery A group of cats that are part of an individual breeding programme. 'Cattery' is also is also the term used to the physical structure that houses a group of cats.

Cattery name A name registered with a cat registry to identify cats bred by a specific breeder. A registered cattery name always appears as a prefix to the names of cats bred by that breeder. It may be added as a suffix to the names of cats owned, but not bred by, that breeder.

Certificate In some cat associations, cats are awarded certificates at shows. Certificates are accumulated in order to obtain titles.

Certified pedigree A pedigree officially issued to a cat by a cat registering association.

Championship The classification by which entire adult cats are entered for competition.

Coat A cat's fur.

Crossbreed The mating of cats of two different breeds. The offspring of such a mating is considered a crossbreed (see Moggy).

Cryptorchid An adult male cat whose testicles have not descended into the scrotal sac. This is viewed as an automatic disqualification point by all registries.

Dam The female parent of a cat.

Disqualification A quality listed in the standard that makes a cat ineligible for show. A cat may also be disqualified on health or behavioural grounds.

Domestic longhair (DLH) A longhaired cat of unknown or mixed parentage.

Domestic shorthair (DSH) A shorthaired cat of unknown or mixed parentage.

Double coat A cat's coat made up of two layers: a top layer and a softer undercoat. This gives the cat extra protection from the cold.

Exhibitor An individual who exhibits cats at a show.

Fancier An individual who keeps, exhibits and breeds pedigree cats.

Hairless cats A cat with very little hair, though not literally hairless. Hairless cats are bred on a defective gene. Their skin is very soft and smooth, however, and the hairless cat's skin often requires more care than a coated cat.

Heat A Queen's oestrus period, during which time she is fertile.

Household pet The term given to cats of mixed or non-pedigree parentage which may be entered in the Household Pet classes at shows. They do not compete against pedigree cats entered in the main part of the show.

Inbreeding The mating of closely related cats to preserve desirable breed qualities. For example, the mating of brother and sister, or father and daughter.

Kitten A young, immature cat. Kittens are shown in their own age group at shows.

Litter One or more kittens produced by a single pregnancy.

Longhair A cat with relatively long fur, often varying in length over different parts of the cat.

Mixed breed A cat of unknown or mixed parentage.

Moggy The slang UK term for mixed breed.

Molly A female cat.

Monorchid An adult male cat that has only one descended testicle. This is a disqualification fault in all associations.

Neuter The term given to the castration of a male cat. A 'neuter' is the show term for a male or female cat that has been neutered.

Odd-eyed A cat with one blue eye and one green, gold or copper eye.

Pedigree A document recognized by a cat registry that records the ancestors of a cat. 'Pedigree' is also the term for a cat with a pedigree.

Prefix The cattery name at the beginning of the cat's name, indicating the breeder's cattery.

Premier The equivalent title to Champion for a neutered adult cat.

Queen An entire, un-spayed female cat.

Registry The governing association for a given country or territory at which cats are registered. The registry has a number of clubs affiliated to it; these clubs may host shows at which registered cats may be shown.

Rex cats These cats have a curly coat. There is a gene responsible for the curliness. They are often called 'Poodle Cats' because of the resemblance in coat to the Poodle.

Ring: An area at a show where judges examine cats to place them in order of merit. A show may have several simultaneous rings.

Semi-longhair A longhaired cat that does not have an extremely long coat.

Shorthair A cat with a relatively short coat.

Show An exhibition of cats, at which the cats are entered and judged for their conformance to breed standards.

Show cat A cat that is exhibited in a show.

Show quality A cat that meets its breed standard closely enough to compete in a show.

Sire The male parent of a litter.

Spay The surgical procedure to remove the reproductive organs of the female cat. A 'spay' is the term for a spayed female cat.

Spray The behaviour, usually of entire tom cats, of urinating to establish his territory.

Standard A description of the body points and breed characteristics and associated criteria by which a cat is judged.

Stud cat An entire male cat that is used for breeding.

Suffix The cattery name at the end of the cat's name, if any, indicating the cattery in which the cat resides.

Title An award earned by a cat that may be added to the cat's name according to the rules of a cat registering association, e.g. Champion (CH).

Tom An un-neutered, entire male cat.

Triple coat A cat's coat made up of three layers. The Siberian Cat's triple coat helps it survive in the coldest of climates. The coat is shed in warmer weather for comfort.

Who's going to lay their claws on the rosette?

It will be a catastrophe if I don't win

I am the cat's whiskers

We're all winning pawsibilities

I'm head and tail above the rest

Best in show

GLOSSARY

All Breed Show A show open to all recognized breeds of pedigree cat at which the cats will be judged against each other.

Any Other Colour (AOC) A class for cats with coat colours not previously covered in a show's schedule.

Any Other Variety (AOV) A class for all cat breeds not previously covered in a show's schedule, sometimes including breeds that are not eligible to compete for titles.

Bloodline A group of related cats from a particular lineage.

Breed standard The ideal characteristics and judging criteria for the breed, as agreed upon by breeders and registries.

Breeder The breeder of a cat is technically the owner of the cat's dam (mother) at the time of mating.

Calling The characteristic vocalizations made by a female cat when in heat.

Cat Fancy The term given to the national or international group of individuals, clubs and registering associations involved with the breeding and showing of cats.

Cattery A group of cats that are part of an individual breeding programme. 'Cattery' is also is also the term used to the physical structure that houses a group of cats.

Cattery name A name registered with a cat registry to identify cats bred by a specific breeder. A registered cattery name always appears as a prefix to the names of cats bred by that breeder. It may be added as a suffix to the names of cats owned, but not bred by, that breeder.

Certificate In some cat associations, cats are awarded certificates at shows. Certificates are accumulated in order to obtain titles.

Certified pedigree A pedigree officially issued to a cat by a cat registering association.

Championship The classification by which entire adult cats are entered for competition.

Coat A cat's fur.

Crossbreed The mating of cats of two different breeds. The offspring of such a mating is considered a crossbreed (see Moggy).

Cryptorchid An adult male cat whose testicles have not descended into the scrotal sac. This is viewed as an automatic disqualification point by all registries.

Dam The female parent of a cat.

Disqualification A quality listed in the standard that makes a cat ineligible for show. A cat may also be disqualified on health or behavioural grounds.

Domestic longhair (DLH) A longhaired cat of unknown or mixed parentage.

Domestic shorthair (DSH) A shorthaired cat of unknown or mixed parentage.

Double coat A cat's coat made up of two layers: a top layer and a softer undercoat. This gives the cat extra protection from the cold.

Exhibitor An individual who exhibits cats at a show.

Fancier An individual who keeps, exhibits and breeds pedigree cats.

Hairless cats A cat with very little hair, though not literally hairless. Hairless cats are bred on a defective gene. Their skin is very soft and smooth, however, and the hairless cat's skin often requires more care than a coated cat.

Heat A Queen's oestrus period, during which time she is fertile.

Household pet The term given to cats of mixed or non-pedigree parentage which may be entered in the Household Pet classes at shows. They do not compete against pedigree cats entered in the main part of the show.

Inbreeding The mating of closely related cats to preserve desirable breed qualities. For example, the mating of brother and sister, or father and daughter.

Kitten A young, immature cat. Kittens are shown in their own age group at shows.

Litter One or more kittens produced by a single pregnancy.

Longhair A cat with relatively long fur, often varying in length over different parts of the cat.

Mixed breed A cat of unknown or mixed parentage.

Moggy The slang UK term for mixed breed.

Molly A female cat.

Monorchid An adult male cat that has only one descended testicle. This is a disqualification fault in all associations.

Neuter The term given to the castration of a male cat. A 'neuter' is the show term for a male or female cat that has been neutered.

Odd-eyed A cat with one blue eye and one green, gold or copper eye.

Pedigree A document recognized by a cat registry that records the ancestors of a cat. 'Pedigree' is also the term for a cat with a pedigree.

Prefix The cattery name at the beginning of the cat's name, indicating the breeder's cattery.

Premier The equivalent title to Champion for a neutered adult cat.

Queen An entire, un-spayed female cat.

Registry The governing association for a given country or territory at which cats are registered. The registry has a number of clubs affiliated to it; these clubs may host shows at which registered cats may be shown.

Rex cats These cats have a curly coat. There is a gene responsible for the curliness. They are often called 'Poodle Cats' because of the resemblance in coat to the Poodle.

Ring: An area at a show where judges examine cats to place them in order of merit. A show may have several simultaneous rings.

Semi-longhair A longhaired cat that does not have an extremely long coat.

Shorthair A cat with a relatively short coat.

Show An exhibition of cats, at which the cats are entered and judged for their conformance to breed standards.

Show cat A cat that is exhibited in a show.

Show quality A cat that meets its breed standard closely enough to compete in a show.

Sire The male parent of a litter.

Spay The surgical procedure to remove the reproductive organs of the female cat. A 'spay' is the term for a spayed female cat.

Spray The behaviour, usually of entire tom cats, of urinating to establish his territory.

Standard A description of the body points and breed characteristics and associated criteria by which a cat is judged.

Stud cat An entire male cat that is used for breeding.

Suffix The cattery name at the end of the cat's name, if any, indicating the cattery in which the cat resides.

Title An award earned by a cat that may be added to the cat's name according to the rules of a cat registering association, e.g. Champion (CH).

Tom An un-neutered, entire male cat.

Triple coat A cat's coat made up of three layers. The Siberian Cat's triple coat helps it survive in the coldest of climates. The coat is shed in warmer weather for comfort.

ASSOCIATIONS

BRITAIN
The Governing Council of the Cat Fancy (GCCF)
5 King's Castle Business Park
The Drove
Bridgwater
Somerset
TA6 4AG
UK
Tel: 0044 (0)1278 427575
www.gccfcats.org

Felis Britannica (FB)
131 Caxton Road
Hoddesdon
Hertfordshire
EN11 9NX
UK
Tel: 0044 (0)7545 824832
www.felisbritannica.org

USA
The Cat Fanciers' Association (CFA)
260 East Main Street
Alliance
OH 44601
USA
Tel: 001 330 680 4070
www.cfa.org

American Cat Fanciers Association (ACFA)
PO Box 1949
Nixa
MO 65714-1949
USA
Tel: 001 417 725 1530
www.acfacat.com

Cat Fanciers' Federation (CFF)
Tel: 001 937 787 9009
www.cffinc.org

AUSTRALIA
Australian Cat Federation (ACF)
PO Box 331
Port Adelaide BC
SA 5015
Australia
Tel: 0061 (0)8 8449 5880
www.acf.asn.au

CANADA
**Canadian Cat Association/
Association Féline Canadienne (CCA-AFC)**
4505 Orbitor Drive
Building 12, Suite 102
Mississauga
ON L4W 4Y4
Canada
Tel: 001 905 232 3481
www.cca-afc.com

NEW ZEALAND
New Zealand Cat Fancy (NZCF)
43 Walker Road West
RD 2
Katikati 3178
New Zealand
Tel: 0064 (0)7 549 2752
www.nzcatfancy.gen.nz

SOUTH AFRICA
The Southern African Cat Council (SACC)
5 Stanmore Road
Kensington
Gauteng
2094
South Africa
Tel: 0027 (0)11 616 7017
www.tsacc.org.za

INTERNATIONAL
Fédération Internationale Féline (FIFe)
fifeweb.org

The International Cat Association (TICA)
PO Box 2684
Harlingen
TX 78551
USA
Tel: 001 956 428 8046
www.tica.org

World Cat Congress (WCC)
www.worldcatcongress.org

World Cat Federation (WCF)
www.wcf-online.de

PICTURE CREDITS

The publisher would like to thank the following for permission to reproduce copyright material: Aceshot1/Shutterstock (page 7), Pete Pahham/Shutterstock (8), Prisma Archivo/Alamy (9), Liszt Collection/Alamy (10) and Hulton-Deutsch Collection/Corbis (11).

AUTHORS' ACKNOWLEDGEMENTS

Darlene Arden
For so many reasons I want to thank my best friend/chosen sister, Sue Janson. For so many practical lessons about cats there is no better teacher than my beloved Chartreux, Aimee. I want to thank my wonderful editor, Tom Kitch, for allowing me to bring another author aboard this project and thanks to Nick Mays for agreeing to co-author this book. And always, always for my mother. I miss her every single day.

Nick Mays
With many thanks to my better half Sheena for her unstinting support and belief, and to Chrissy Russell and Sally E. Bahner for much needed advice. Also huge thanks to Darlene Arden for wanting me on board as co-author and to Tom Kitch at Ivy for his supreme patience and tolerance when being guided through the foibles of the Fancy. I'd also like to thank Olly, a fine feline gent who started my love of cats and who tolerated the attentions of the irritating 6-year-old me and still had a purr for me when he reached the ripe old age of 19.

PUBLISHER'S ACKNOWLEDGEMENTS

We would like to thank Lisa Aggett and all of the other organizers of the Supreme Cat Show, Birmingham, and Jeannine Parfitt and all of her team at the TICA in Bloom show, Oxford, for all their help with setting up our photoshoots and making us feel so welcome at the shows. We would also like to thank Mark Goadby (GCCF), Vickie Fisher (TICA) and Roeann Fulkerson (CFA) for their assistance with the breed standards.

THE CATS

We would like to thank all of the following cat owners and breeders who allowed us to photograph their cats for this book.

Abyssinian Amy-May Thomson & Mandy Rainbow
Australian Mist Tricia Bristow
Bengal Di Cheal
Birman Jenny Bush
Bombay JJ McCarten
British Shorthair Dylan Taylor
Burmese Patricia Tegg
Burmilla Louise Mitchell
Chartreux Ludovic Lebon
Cornish Rex Robert Dunne
Cymric/Longhaired Manx Mrs S Church
Devon Rex Stanley Bryant
Egyptian Mau Lizzie Edge
Exotic Shorthair Sarah Hemsley
Himalayan/Colourpoint Persian Douglas D'Abate
Khao Manee Chrissy Russell
Korat Mrs Judy East
Kurilian Bobtail Maria Bunina
LaPerm Edwina Sipos
Maine Coon Sue Lyle
Manx Mrs S Church
Nebelung Kristi Stewart
Norwegian Forest Cat Delsa Rudge
Ocicat Lorraine Parry
Oriental Kate Wells-McCulloch
Persian Marie Hill
Ragdoll Jason Lombard-Jordan & Andrew Jordan-Lombard
Russian Blue (GCCF) Karen Hettmann
Russian Blue (TICA) Jeannine Parfitt
Selkirk Rex Karen Winn
Siamese Becky Poole
Siberian James & Sue Dear
Singapura Marcia Owen
Snowshoe Kelly Cruse
Sokoke CM Payne
Somali Kathy Hines
Sphynx Jane Haggar
Tiffanie Heather McRae
Tonkinese Louise O'Shea
Turkish Van Jason Lombard-Jordan & Andrew Jordan-Lombard

INDEX